In memory of
Rico Montenero,
grandfather of
Kelly and Mike
Montenero.

# THE MOON OF THE
## MOLES

# THE THIRTEEN MOONS

The Moon of the Owls (JANUARY)

The Moon of the Bears (FEBRUARY)

The Moon of the Salamanders (MARCH)

The Moon of the Chickarees (APRIL)

The Moon of the Monarch Butterflies (MAY)

The Moon of the Fox Pups (JUNE)

The Moon of the Wild Pigs (JULY)

The Moon of the Mountain Lions (AUGUST)

The Moon of the Deer (SEPTEMBER)

The Moon of the Alligators (OCTOBER)

The Moon of the Gray Wolves (NOVEMBER)

The Moon of the Winter Bird (DECEMBER)

The Moon of the Moles (DECEMBER–JANUARY)

NEW EDITION    THE THIRTEEN MOONS

# THE MOON OF THE
# MOLES

BY JEAN CRAIGHEAD GEORGE

ILLUSTRATED BY MICHAEL ROTHMAN

HarperCollins*Publishers*

The illustrations in this book were painted with acrylic
on archival polyester.

The Moon of the Moles
Text copyright © 1969, 1992 by Jean Craighead George
Illustrations copyright © 1992 by Michael Rothman

Typography by Al Cetta
1 2 3 4 5 6 7 8 9 10
NEW EDITION

Library of Congress Cataloging-in-Publication Data
George, Jean Craighead, date
    The moon of the moles / Jean Craighead George ; illustrated by
Michael Rothman.—New ed.
        p.      cm. — (The Thirteen moons)
    Summary: During December and January, a young mole in
Kansas spends her waking hours searching for food in her network
of underground tunnels.
    ISBN 0-06-020258-0. — ISBN 0-06-020259-9 (lib. bdg.)
    1. Moles (Animals)—Juvenile literature.    2. Moles (Animals)—
Kansas—Juvenile literature.    [1. Moles (Animals).]    I. Rothman,
Michael, ill.    II. Title.    III. Series: George, Jean Craighead, date,
Thirteen moons (HarperCollins)
QL795.M57G46    1992                                    91-14535
599.3´3—dc20                                                  CIP
                                                                      AC  r91

## Why is this series called The Thirteen Moons?

Each year there are either thirteen full moons or thirteen new moons. This series of books is named in their honor.

Our culture, which bases its calendar year on sun-time, has no names for the thirteen moons. I have named the thirteen lunar months after thirteen North American animals. Primarily night prowlers, these animals, at a particular time of the year in a particular place, do wondrous things. The places are known to you, but the animal moon names are not because I made them up. So that you can place them on our sun calendar, I have identified them with the names of our months. When I ran out of these, I gave the thirteenth moon, the Moon of the Moles, the expandable name December-January.

Fortunately, the animals do not need calendars, for names or no names, sun-time or moon-time, they follow their own inner clocks.

—JEAN CRAIGHEAD GEORGE

IN A COZY BEDCHAMBER under the earth, an Eastern mole was awakened by a violent tremor. She was no bigger than a child's hand. She lifted her cone-shaped and furless nose from her belly fur and instantly got to her four feet. The palms of her front feet, which are broader than they are long and tipped with strong claws, were turned outward for digging. But she did not dig. She ran. Alarmed by the shaking of the earth, the silvery-brown mole sped along one of her many tunnels in total darkness. As abruptly as the tremors had begun, they stopped. The mole breathed deeply and began to relax.

Above the earth, a full moon was circling the planet for the thirteenth time of the year. It was the moon of winter darkness in the Northern Hemisphere, the moon of the moles. For moles, darkness is life.

The little mole lived under a parcel of the Great Plains of North America—an expanse of flat land that lies like a belt down the middle of the continent from northern Canada to southern Texas. It slopes gently eastward from the Rocky Mountains for four hundred miles. In Canada the Great Plains include parts of Alberta and Saskatchewan. In the United States they include eastern Montana, Wyoming, Colorado, and New Mexico, parts of Oklahoma and Texas; and western North and South Dakota, Nebraska, and Kansas. The mole was two feet below the surface of the eastern edge of the plains near Crooked Creek, eleven miles from Montezuma, Kansas.

The Great Plains are semiarid. About twenty inches of rain a year falls on this land of grass, wind, and flatness. Trees, unless planted by humans, grow only in protected riverbeds. Once a territory of wild grasses where the buffalo and Native Americans thrived together, the great belt is now blocked off into farms and ranches. Wheat, milo, and corn are grown in the eastern plains. Cattle and sheep graze the plains of the west, intermingling with pronghorns, deer, and coyotes.

When the moon of December-January shone down on the Great Plains, the smaller mammals—the prairie dogs, voles, and ground squirrels—were in their earthen beds beneath the frost line. Some were hibernating until spring. Others were snoozing through the December-January darkness, awakening now and then to eat and stretch. The mole, however, was up and

about, for she was as busy in winter as she was in summer, when the sun warmed her subterranean acre of Kansas.

The silvery mole did not relax long. The tremors over, and her fears conquered, she went to work. The frost had come far down into the ground during the night. Ice crystals crackled from the roof of her tunnel.

On the snowy ground above her, a coyote walked. A crow called to his mate, and a cotton-tail chewed on a raspberry bud. The mole did not know about these things, for she had never been out of the ground. Born in May in a nest of grass under a rancher's vegetable garden a mile away, she had become acquainted with plump radishes, but not their green tops. She knew tomato roots, but not their red fruits. Her world was underground. She was a digger, a member of the family Talpidae, who live under United States soil from coast to coast, and from southeastern Canada to the Gulf of Mexico. Seven species make up the family in North America, each differing from the others in accordance with the type of soil it lives in. The star-nosed mole likes damp meadows, moist woods, and bogs; the hairy-tailed mole seeks the well-drained soils of woodlands; and the mole of Montezuma, Kansas, *Scalopus aquaticus*, and her kin inhabit the loose soils of meadows, pastures, and open woodlands. The others like slightly different soils, but all live underground.

When she was a month old, the mole had left her mother and two brothers and had followed a family labyrinth to the end of the garden. With a bushel of dirt, she had closed the route back to her home, turned west, and excavated a tunnel far out under the wheat field. Her tunnel was neat and small, about one and a half inches wide and one

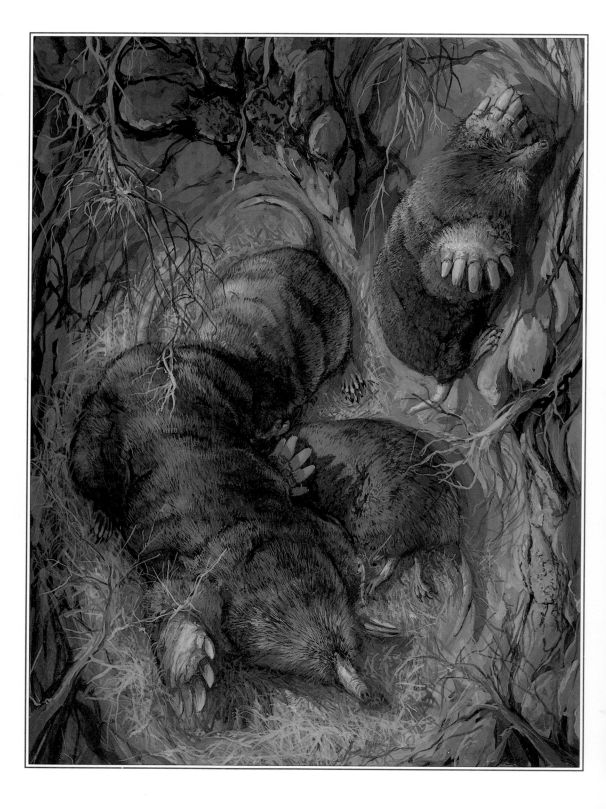

inch high. After digging for several days, she had come to the rich loam along Crooked Creek. She smelled its many insects and worms and was pleased. Still unaware of the sun and the moon, she had begun her solitary life as an adult mole.

After settling down, she had carved a round chamber beneath a rock buried in the creek bank. She had filled it with rootlets and bits of root bark and woven them into a bed. Then she had excavated five runways from this central station until she had four miles of major tunnels. The Wheat-Root Run wound under the field. The Creek Run ran along the bank of Crooked Creek. The Cottonwood Run led in and around the roots of the cottonwood trees, and the Road Run went through soft loam and grass roots to the edge of the human-made country road. The Bridge Run, her favorite, tunneled off to a white-grub (beetle larva) community and on to the worm-filled soil near the bridge. These she relished, for she was an insectivore as well as a digger.

The mole ran her tunnels without seeing. Moles have lived in the ground for so long that their eyes have become functionless. The eyes are mere specks on either side of the mole's head, too small to register anything but light and dark. Skin grows over them. Many moles live their entire lives—one to three years—without experiencing more than a pale ray of light. Certainly this mole had not seen sunshine or moonshine, for she had dug deep.

Lack of sight did not bother the mole. She had inherited from her ancestors a highly developed sense of smell. She could "see," so to speak, with her nose.

As she ran along her tunnel this day, the scent of ice crystals in the ground speckled the darkness with chemical shapes. A worm appeared in the

smelling part of her brain. She dug through the earth to it as if she could see it. She ate.

Her lightless "day" would last three hours; then she would sleep for five hours. A twenty-four-hour day on top of the earth was three mole days.

Although there is no night and day under the ground, just the times the mole is awake and asleep, there are seasons. The mole knew it was winter from the behavior of the roots. They do not die like the surface plants, they simply change their activities. The winter-wheat roots that had come down into the mole's tunnel soon after the crops were planted in September were no longer writhing as they do in the growing season, but were creeping and seeking. They were taking up minerals and water and holding them in their storage cells below the frost line. The roots were growing at their tips as they moved away from the cold. They were full and stiff with the food they had collected and stored for the spring revival of leaves. Fat roots meant winter to the mole.

The earth shook again. The mole sniffed, but could not "see" what was disturbing her world. Dirt fell into her tunnels, and a root, searching for soil and food, swung down and touched her nose. She nipped it flush with her ceiling and, nervous about the tremors again, paused to collect herself by brushing her fur. As soft as bird down, her mantle could be pushed backward, forward, sideways, or straight up. This kind of fur was necessary for her subterranean way of life. She could run forward in her tight tunnels, back up, or turn around without being made uncomfortable by rumpled fur. Mole fur has no wrong way to be brushed.

When she heard only silence for a while, she

stopped grooming herself and left the rest of the brushing and combing to the walls of her tunnels. She was very hungry. Moles have to eat food in amounts equal to their body weight—an ounce and a half—each day.

Turning away from the tremor, she hurried along the Wheat-Root Run. Hardly had she gone a hundred feet when she came to a blocked tunnel to the outside world. She had made this while digging the run. When she had accumulated a large pile of dirt, she had dug a shaft to the surface. Then she had turned around and, passing the dirt under her belly to her hind feet, had kicked it up the shaft. The dirt had shot out onto the field above and piled up in a mound. Under the December-January moon, the mole mounds of soil from subterranean Kansas were still evident. Plants would flourish in them in spring, for moles not only aerate the soil, they also bring

deep, rich loam to the surface.

The mole sniffed around her shaft—now blocked with loose dirt—smelled no food, and went down the Bridge Run, which was deeper and warmer. A few hundred feet later she came upon six large worms. They had begun to move downward around two in the morning, burrowed through the mole's ceiling, and fallen to her floor. She pounced upon them and ate with great relish.

She continued along the Bridge Run, stepping with her front feet and pushing with her hind feet. Her rear feet worked like pistons moving straight up and down. The narrow pelvis of the mole permits its hind legs to pump without interference from hips, a perfect design for someone living in a tunnel.

Her pistonlike stride gave the mole considerable speed. She moved swiftly, devouring every worm and beetle larva she came upon. After two hours of running and eating, she stopped at a boulder. It marked the end of her home range and the beginning of another mole's property—a male's. He had broken into her tunnel one day last autumn. She had been furious at him and had walled him off with a bushel of dirt. Today she did not feel so antagonistic toward him. February, the breeding season of the moles, was not far off. Without knowing why, she took down a portion of the barrier and listened for her neighbor. Then she turned around by folding her supple spine into a U and hurried back to her bedchamber. She rested briefly before taking off for the Road Run, looking for more food.

For several hours she dug and ate grubs, as well as a spider and a centipede. When her day was almost over, she squeezed through a particularly narrow, steep part of the Road Run to a patch of loose dirt. With her nimble feet she opened the door to another bedchamber. This was an emergency retreat some six inches deeper than her central station, and therefore warmer. Arranging its root cuttings over and around her with her feet and nose, she sat on her haunches and tucked her nose into her tail. Almost instantly she was asleep. The mole's day was done.

Whatever the mole did, she did wholeheartedly. Now she slept with a vengeance. So deeply was she sleeping that she did not hear the next series of tremors down by Crooked Creek, made by humans driving stakes into the ground.

Five hours later she awoke and poked her pointed nose into her tunnel. She breathed deeply of the underground air. The air came from the spaces between the grains of soil, and was changed and renewed.

The fat nymph of a cicada appeared in the

mole's nose-eyes. It was above her head, curled like a shrimp and chewing on the roots of a sunflower. She stood on her hind feet and dug it out of the ceiling, sniffed, and found another.

Feeling energetic now, she set out for the Creek Run. In a quarter of a mile she came to a cluster of buffalo-grass roots that marked the closed entrance to one of her summer tunnels. These runs lay so close to the surface, they were actually ridges above ground. In the vegetable garden where she had been born, the farmer trampled them and complained about moles.

Since this was the season of fat roots, the mole had no desire to work near the cold surface. She dug down.

In one minute she had gone six inches, found thirteen large earthworms, and eaten them all. Having consumed her ounce of food for the day, she went back to her winter bedchamber.

The next solar day on top of the earth began in the middle of the mole's night. A loud grating awoke her. Her body shook, the rootlets in her bedchamber shifted. She scraped back her nest material and, placing her feet lightly on the bare ground, listened through the circle of hairs around each palm. Through these she could hear—the mole has no external ears, just a ring of cartilage buried in the fur. Ears would be a hindrance to a creature that runs through narrow underground tunnels. Over the eons as the mole evolved, its ears had become useless and vanished. Sound-sensitive hairs had developed on its feet and on its short, almost bare tail.

The earth rumbled again. The rumbling came from close overhead. She sped to her most distant tunnel, the Cottonwood Run.

When her short-lived fear subsided, she slowed down to a waddle. The good smell of food was in the soil, and she dug.

As she worked, a hollowness sounded on the hairs around her palms. She was coming to a stranger's tunnel. She dug more carefully. It could belong to a mole-eating coyote or badger. With precision she carved the wall to cardboard thinness and listened with her palms. The new tunnel was small and narrow. Such a run could belong only to a pocket gopher or ground squirrel. These animals were friends, not enemies. With her nose, the mole broke open the tunnel and stepped in.

Her nose told her it belonged to a female thirteen-lined ground squirrel. It also told her the labyrinth was rich with worms that were feeding on leaf bits and grass blades brought into the gallery by this chipmunklike squirrel of the plains.

The colorful ground squirrel was fast asleep in her chamber at the end of a long tunnel. She had

closed her door to the surface with grass and leaves in October and retreated into her labyrinth to sleep for weeks. Occasionally she awakened to eat, but not this day. The mole was free to investigate the ground squirrel's pantry of seeds. They came from sunflowers, clover, wheat, ragweed, bristle grass, and prickly-pear plants on the surface of the earth. All were strangers to the mole. She touched them with her palms, and an image of tiny underground river stones came to mind.

The mole took advantage of the squirrel's torpor and hurried through the squirrel's network of trails, eating the earthworms that had fallen into it and investigating her twenty-five feet of diggings. When the mole's three-hour day was over, she ran toward home. She could hear her nails click against the hard-packed soil of the ground squirrel's burrow.

As she arrived back at the hole where she had broken into the ground squirrel's runway, she smelled water. The squirrel's home was over a layer of gravel, an aquifer that held glacial water in the spaces between the stones. The water had been moving about a foot a year for ten thousand years. It ran slowly downhill through the vast gravel beds that lie in layers under the plains toward the Gulf of Mexico. Farmers and ranchers on the Great Plains dig wells down to this "ground water" and pump it to the surface for irrigation and drinking.

The smell of water made the mole thirsty. She scooped a hole in the gravel. The hole quickly filled with cool, clear water, and she sipped the refreshment. As her day came to an end, she sealed the break in the wall and scurried to her winter bedchamber. Buried in her rootlet snippings, she fell asleep.

The mole was awakened again by the earth tremors. She got up, put her feet on the floor of her tunnel, and, feeling the rumblings to the west, ran down her Road Run and north.

When she reached an iron fence post in the ground, she stopped and placed a front foot on it. It was her weather vane—it told her about the surface. The post was cold and shaking violently, not from the wind but from a great moving object that was hitting the post. She made a U-turn and headed off to her Creek Run.

In the rich loam by the creek she found many more earthworms but did not eat them. She needed sleep more than food. Digging herself a makeshift bedchamber away from the noise, she curled up. The soil by the stream was a populated place during the moon of December-January. The mole dropped off to sleep listening to a moth pupa wiggle and a Japanese beetle larva chew.

She slept late the next mole day, then hunted her mile of Creek Run and checked for food in the Cottonwood Run. Among the roots she came upon a colony of ants. They were crossing her tunnel as they carried their larvae from the cold ground near the surface to their deepest nursery beneath a boulder. The descending frost was driving them downward. The mole ate a few larvae, then began a new tunnel at the end of her Cottonwood Run, far from the source of the earth tremors.

For the next two mole days she did not hear the rumblings. She relaxed, ran all her tunnels again, slept well, and ate heartily. She could not know that it was Sunday in the human world, and that the people who were making the earth shake were on their holiday.

That mole morning she smelled strawberry roots. Their odor carries far enough through the

soil for these plants to stake out their territory with a strong scent. Other roots turn away from their chemicals and leave the soil to them. The mole found an active strawberry rootlet creeping into her tunnel. With a nip she ate its growing tip, on which hundreds of little hairs were clustered. These were the "mouths" that took in water and minerals. When the tip grew on beyond the mouths, they would vanish, and new ones would emerge around the new tip.

The strawberry root was a warning to the mole. The freeze was deepening. She made a U-turn and hurried to a musty layer of earth. It was made up of plant life that had once grown by the creek. As the vegetation decomposed, it became peat and gave off heat. The mole dug into this warm layer and made a Peat Run to protect herself against the cold and the noise.

The next mole day she broke into the winter

home of a female bullfrog. The amphibian was hibernating—her front feet pulled up and under her chin, her back feet tucked under her cold belly. The frog's eyes were open, for she had no lids to close. A thin, transparent membrane protected them from dirt and grit. The mole kicked soil over the frog as she dug on, searching for grubs and worms.

That mole night she fell asleep listening with her feet to the crackle of a box elder's roots as they braced the tree against a lashing winter wind coming across the Great Plains.

Five hours later she scurried back to the Creek Run. Finding only a few worms, she dug furiously toward a gathering of white grubs and broke into the den of a pocket gopher. The gopher was awake and shifting her food from one pantry to another. She scolded the mole so ferociously that the little blind mole dug into the floor, flipped dirt on herself, and hid. The gopher screamed louder. Knowing that the mole would do her no harm, she then backed away and began moving supplies again.

The mole waited until the gopher ran off to a distant gallery. Then she uncovered herself, repaired the break in the gopher's wall, and ran a mile along the Bridge Run. Again the earth shook. The mole fled to her Cottonwood Run and as far down it as she could get.

The next day she began another tunnel off the Wheat-Root Run that would take her still farther away from the earth tremors. While she was kicking dirt up a shaft, she smelled a coyote. He was digging down toward her, snapping hungrily.

Terrified, the mole sprayed the coyote with her protective scent, an acrid musk that burns the nose and eyes. The scent did no good. It was December-January; the gophers and ground

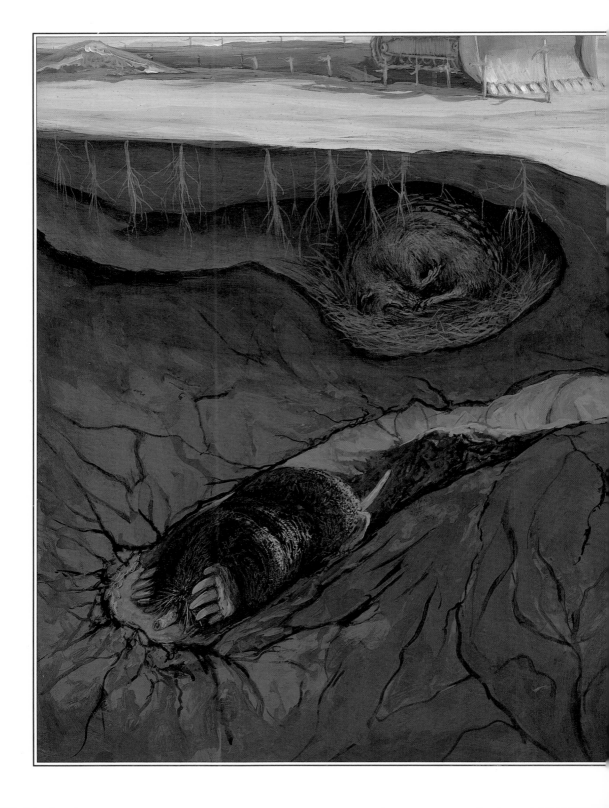

squirrels were all underground. The coyote was terribly hungry. He dug on. The mole fled to the creek. The coyote heard her, pounced, and dug again. She ran the other way. He pounced and dug again, this time cutting her off from her runs. She would not live long without them. She needed the runs to provide enough food for her ferocious hunger.

She did not stop to think about that. She dug straight down, faster than the coyote could dig, then west, and with a snort broke into her Wheat-Root Run. She could run faster in her tunnel than the coyote could pounce and dig. In an instant she was in her main bedchamber. The coyote gave up when he could no longer smell her.

The next mole day the ground was quiet, and she was able to repair the Creek Run, which had collapsed under the tremors. She was working energetically—when suddenly she was on top of the earth. Her tunnel had been cut into and exposed.

The mole was terrified. No walls hugged her, no soil scents gave her a sense of direction. The air was loose and vast. She felt blindly for the hole she had just left but could not find it. Clinging to a stone that smelled of herself, she lifted her nose. The odor of steel and grease burned her nostrils. The smell went so high, she could not find its end. She was against the wheel of the huge machine that was cutting a swath for a superhighway across Kansas. The mole's loamy home by the river was threatened.

She stood very still. Animal scents blew up from the creek bed. A musky mink was fishing in the cold. A white-tailed deer was bedded down in the cottonwoods. A badger was digging for a gopher. From every direction came the smell of birds: pheasants in the wheat field, crows in the

willows, juncos in the windbreak of the box elders.

Then she looked up. Her head glowed. Sparks crackled in her brain. The light from the full moon of December-January fell onto her tiny eyes, and the mole of Crooked Creek saw it.

For a long time she looked at the moon. Then a wind brought the scent of her own trail. She put her nose down and followed it. Within a few feet she smelled the sweet odor of her hole. She dove in, closed the machine-made rip with two bushels of dirt, and sat still.

As she did, a pleasant afterglow burned on her feeble retinas, and again she saw the moon of the moles, the thirteenth moon of the year, shining down on all the Earth's beautiful creatures.

# Bibliography

*Animal Kingdom: The Illustrated Encyclopedia.* Vol. 5, page 26. Suffern, NY: Danbury Press, 1972.

Bailey, Jill. *Discovering Shrews, Moles and Voles.* New York: Bookwright Press, 1989.

Burt, William H., and Richard P. Grossenheider. *A Field Guide to the Mammals.* The Petersen Field Guide Series. Boston: Houghton Mifflin Company, 1976.

Mellanby, Kenneth. *The Mole.* New York: Taplinger Publishing Co. Inc., 1977.

Ripper, Charles L. *Moles and Shrews.* New York: William Morrow and Company, Inc., 1957.

*The World Book Encyclopedia.* Vol. 13, page 575. Chicago: World Book, Inc., 1986.

# Index

ants, 35
aquifer, 33

badgers, 30, 43
beetles, 17, 25, 34, 35, 38
box elder trees, 38, 45
bristle grass, 32
buffalo grass, 27
bullfrogs, 38

centipedes, 25
cicadas, 26–27
clover, 32
cottonwood trees, 17
coyotes, 12, 14, 30, 39, 42
crows, 14, 43, 45

deer, 12, 43

Great Plains, 11–12, 33, 38
ground squirrels, 12, 30, 32–33, 42
grubs, 17, 25, 38

hibernation, 12, 32, 38

insects, 17, 18

juncos, 45

minks, 43

moles
    life span, 18
    physical characteristics, 9, 18, 21, 22, 24, 29, 39
    species, 15
    tunneling, 14–15, 17–18, 21, 22, 24, 25, 26, 29, 32, 34, 35, 37, 38, 39, 42
moths, 34

pheasants, 43
pocket gophers, 30, 38–39, 43
prairie dogs, 12
prickly pears, 32
pronghorns, 12

ragweed, 32
raspberries, 14
roots, 20–21, 26, 27, 33, 35, 37

spiders, 25
strawberries, 35
sunflowers, 27, 32

voles, 12

wheat, 12, 15, 20–21, 32, 43
willow trees, 45
worms, 17, 18, 20, 24, 25, 27, 30, 32, 34, 38